BLACK EYES *and*
a Pure Heart

BLACK EYES *and*
a Pure Heart

VANESSA FARR

J. Kenkade
PUBLISHING
LITTLE ROCK, ARKANSAS

Black Eyes and a Pure Heart
Copyright © 2017 Vanessa Farr

J. Kenkade Publishing
5920 Highway 5 N Ste. 7
Bryant, AR 72022
www.jkenkadepublishing.com
@jkenkadepublishing

J. Kenkade Publishing is a registered trademark.
Printed in the United States of America

This book recounts actual events in the life of Vanessa Farr according to the author's recollection and perspective. Some of the identifying details may have been changed to respect the privacy of those involved.

The views expressed in this book are those of the author and do not necessarily reflect the views of Publisher.

TABLE OF CONTENTS

Chapter 1
START OF LIFE

Y ou better not be pregnant! Mama shouted standing over me with her finger in my face. "You're only 17." Her voice may have reflected her anger, but in her eyes, I could see utter disappointment and hurt.

"What about your goals? What about finishing high school?"

There were so many questions that I didn't have the answer to. She went silent and started pacing the room. I sat still, fear paralyzing me on the couch. I was waiting to see what she was going to do next.

I watched her move back and forth across the room, my eyes never leaving her face. Then she came to a sudden stop, and it looked like a light came on inside her mind.

"You can't stay here."

She said it with such finality that my heart began to pound its way through my rib cage.

"No, you can't stay here," she repeated.

"I'm not going to take care of you and a baby. Since you want to run around and act all grown, you're going to have to stand on your own two feet like a real grown woman. You got to get out."

My limbs, which had been paralyzed just a moment before, lost all their composure and seemed to melt away.

"But Mama, I don't have anywhere else to go. You know that."

My eyes began to pool with unshed tears. They were pleading for her mercy, but she wasn't moved by my fears, nor my tears.

"Shawn, I don't know what to tell you. You brought this on yourself. Now, you can either get out, or get an abortion."

She turned and walked out of the room, abruptly ending our conversation before I was ready.

I was so confused and didn't have the first clue of what I was going to do, but I knew I was not going to get rid of my baby. That was out of the question. This day had been overwhelming to say the least.

First, I went to the doctor to confirm what the pregnancy test said. When she said those words I had been dreading since I walked into her office, my mind raced with the thoughts of my next move.

She too had given the option of abortion, but I couldn't hear a word she said after it was confirmed that I was pregnant. Everything seemed to mesh together, and for a moment, I was blotted out of the world—lost in the space of nothingness. I was the one thing my mother had always taught me not to be. *A statistic.* Another under-aged black girl with a baby.

How long had I watched Mama work hard to keep a roof over my head?

How many times had I heard her preach to me about not ending up being mother *and* father to a child?

All my life.

She told me these things as far back as I could remember, but now… here I was doing exactly what she told me not to do.

The tears came pouring from me like a

fountain, and my doctor tried to offer comfort, but there was no way she was going to understand how much of a disappointment I was to not only my family, but to myself. If Mama put me out, I was going to have to rely on welfare; yet another statistic I would fall under, while perpetuating

I was the one thing my mother had always taught me not to be. Another under-aged black girl with a baby.

the stereotype that they so easily showed on TV of one more black girl in the system. I thought about Daddy fighting for our country's freedom in the war and sending me down to Texas in the meantime to live with Mama so I could be safe. But Mama couldn't protect me from sneaking around and having sex. I fell into the wrong crowd and started drinking, doing things I knew my parents wouldn't approve of, and trying to fill an emptiness that those things consistently failed to fill.

Mama reappeared in the room with suitcases loaded down with my clothes.

"Come on Shawn. Get your stuff. You must get the hell out of here. I can't have you staying here with another mouth to feed. *My husband would not approve. He didn't want you here in the first place."*

I knew she said that I was going to have to leave, but I didn't really believe it until I saw my bags in her hand.

How could she be so cruel?

Was I not her baby? My heart hurt with the agony of realizing that she had chosen her husband over me... *again*.

In the middle of all the commotion of getting my bags packed and out the door, she did offer a small "olive branch".

"Call your grandfather. Maybe he'll take you in."

But instead of seeing her offer as a lifeline, I was put off by her gall—offended that she was so willing to get rid of me.

"He's too old, Mama. Why would he take me in? I don't understand how you can just throw me away like this. I'm your child!"

My words came out louder than I had expected them to, and the heat from the palm of Mama's hand across my face cued me into it. Without another word, Mama sat my bags outside the door and then walked back to her room. I could hear the thunderous roar of her bedroom door as it slammed shut. I sat in a stupor trying to gather my thoughts and what was left of my dignity. If I did get rid of this baby like Mama and the doctor recommended, I could go back to living a normal life again and attend college like I had planned.

Maybe they were both right.

I would be giving up my future if I went through with this pregnancy. Things were already so uncertain, and I didn't have another source of income outside of my parents. I began to lean in the direction of accepting my mother's advice when I felt a flutter in my stomach—kind of like a butterfly coming to life. It was my baby moving inside of me.

Immediately, those thoughts of me getting rid of the life growing inside me were fleeting. I reached down and cuddled my stomach, as if the baby were already here sitting in my lap. This child hadn't asked to come into this world. There was no way I could punish him for a choice his father and I had willingly made when we lay down together.

I called Granddad, told him what was going on, and he came without hesitation. When the doorbell rang, Mama didn't even bother to come out of her room, so I pulled myself up from the sofa and answered the door. His smile was warm, and his embrace so welcoming. I let go of all my fears right there on his shoulder, and he held me until I emptied myself of tears. Then he picked up my things from the porch where they still sat waiting and loaded them into the back of his car.

On our way to his house, he reassured me that I could stay for however long I needed, and he would help the best way he could. He also told me about an open position down at the corner store. They needed a cashier right away just like I needed a job right away. This would be my first stop in the morning, before going over to tell the baby's father the big news.

I looked over at my grandfather while he drove us across town and thought, *"Here is a 65-year-old man willing to give up his space, resources, and time to help his grandchild out."*

He noticed me watching him and seemed to be reading my thoughts.

"I promised your Granny before she passed that I would always be here to take care of you guys, and I don't intend on breaking it now."

Grandad looked back over at me and placed his hand on top of mine, giving it a reassuring squeeze before returning to the steering wheel. Thinking about my Granny brought more tears to my eyes. I was so young when she died that I barely remembered her. Grandad did his best to keep her memory alive, but I wanted to see her face. I wanted to hear her voice and remember how her soft hands felt against my skin. She and my uncle had passed away within months of each other. Her family always said her heart just couldn't take losing her only son, and just gave out.

Grandad lived in what most would call "the hood," but there were still children who played carelessly in the street without fear of being shot. There were still weekend cookouts where all the neighbors would come together and fellowship. Everyone knew your name and took care of you as if you were a member of their own family. To the outside world, it may have been the hood, but for Grandad and now me, it would be home.

We walked through the door into his apartment, and Grandad seemed kind of ashamed.

"It's not much, but it's home."

He moved to the side, so I could enter. I gave him a weak smile in hopes that it would be enough to let him know I was grateful for whatever he had to offer.

When I entered, a strong odor invaded my nose. Grandad was a bachelor, so I didn't expect much in the way of neatness. But when I walked in and saw the odor's source, on top of the roaches peeking out from behind his furniture, I knew I had my work cut out for me.

There was one condition my grandfather left me with before retiring to his room. He made me promise that I would finish school. Of course, I promised him, and kissed him on the forehead as a seal of guarantee. When he left the room, I plopped down on the couch wondering where to get started, but even more, wondering how I was going to tell Troy about the pregnancy. He was the baby's father and deserved to know, but would he be a good father and step up to his responsibilities?

My mind was racing. I didn't know what to do or where to start. I got dressed for work before my Granddad dropped me off.

As I was getting out of the car, he said, "Little girl, only the strong survive. Hold your head up. Papa's here with you."

I smiled, closed the car door and told him, "Thanks," as I turned to walk into my job.

It made me feel better to have him in my corner. I clocked in and showed my supervisor my doctor notice. He looked and as he was reading it, asked if I was going to keep it.

I stated, "Yes."

He shook his head and said, "Shawn, you have your whole life ahead of you, and a baby is going to slow you down. If you need help to get rid of the baby, I will help you out."

I looked at him and said, "Okay, I will think about it, and I will let you know."

He hugged me, and I walked to my register. I waived the next customer over to my register, and some woman came up to me. She was smiling, and she looked and asked me how far along I was.

I paused and asked, "How did you know I was pregnant?"

She smiled and asked again. I told her. She asked if I was going to keep it. I told her I didn't know. She didn't have many things to ring up, so when I told her the total, she gave me $100, told me to take out what was owed, and said I could keep the change.

As she grabbed her bags, she looked at me and said, "Ms. Shawn," (I'm guessing she looked at my name tag), "God blessed you with a gift. Make sure you take care of it."

She smiled and walked away. I looked at the

next customer and started working, but what she said to me stuck with me until this day. My baby daddy (BD) Troy came and picked me up from work that night.

He looked at me and said, "Shawn, are you going to keep it?"

I told him, "Yes, I'm going to keep my blessing."

He said, "Shawn, I'm not ready to settle down like that just yet."

When I heard those words, everything I heard from my mom and the doctor resurfaced. I started thinking I was stupid and that I didn't deserve this blessing in my stomach, but deep down I knew God didn't make mistakes. Yeah, I was hurt that he was saying that because at first, he was saying that he only wanted to be with me and now he's not ready to "settle down like that,"

In my head, I was like, *"He's bullshitting, and he got me messed up. We laid down and made this baby together. We gonna take care of this baby together. My child needs to wake up and see mommy and daddy every day."* So, I didn't give a care about what he was saying, honestly. I didn't stay far from my job, so as he was pulling up in the parking lot, I was trying to hide the fact that he had hurt my feelings by saying he was not ready to settle down, but I couldn't. The expression was on my face. He didn't say anything, and he let me get out the car without making sure I made it home. Normally, he would open my car door, walk me to my door, and give me a kiss, but not that night.

I walked in the house. My Granddad had cooked. I ate and showered. While I was in the shower, I was thinking about what my supervisor said about helping me get rid of the baby. Once that thought came in my head, I felt my baby kick for the first time. I just smiled. Feeling him kicking warmed my heart. I just started rubbing my stomach, and I got this urge that I just couldn't wait to hold my baby; but most of all, see what was growing inside of me. I got out of the shower, and I went to my Granddad to tell him about the baby kicking and moving, but he had already fallen asleep.

My Granddad lived a pretty simple life. He used to always say, "Live." He was living his life in the slow lane, laughing. He was a smart, mean old man, though. A couple of months went by, and my sister Denise was by my side more than usual. No matter what, she was always there. I didn't grow up with my sister in the same household, but that never broke our bond. My sister has always stayed with my mom until this day.

It is known that my sister is her favorite child. When I was younger, I used to feel unloved by my mom. She was willing to let me stay with anyone, but she was always overprotective of my little sister, and it used to make me feel like she didn't always like me around her. But I just got used to it and stopped allowing it to bother me.

On November 9, 2006, I was walking home from school, and that day was not like other days. I was sick and in pain more than usual, but I didn't pay the pain no mind because my doctor warned me about Braxton Hicks contractions and told me that morning at my last appointment that I hadn't yet dilated. As I was getting off the bus, liquid was coming down my leg, and I was feeling sharp pains like I'd never felt before. My sister wasn't there like she normally was, so I called her, and she said she was coming. I bent over crying, and my bus driver called the paramedics. They came fast, and my sister didn't make it to me in time.

When I got to the hospital, I heard them saying that I was in labor and that my water broke. My eyes got big as heck.

I was like, *"What the hell? I just went to the doctor. He said it wasn't time."*

I became very nervous and thought, *"The wait is over."*

I was about to be a mommy, but most of all, I was about to meet the most important person in my life. I had turned 18 in July, so I was basically an adult. But was I really ready to take care of a child? I just started praying as well as panicking. As I was being hooked up to the machine to check the baby's heart rate and my blood pressure, I heard a loud woman entering my room.

Boom!

It was my mother, and she was drunk as heck—sloppy drunk at that—and saying, "Where is the nigga that did this to your stupid butt?!"

I told her I had already called him, and he was on his way.

She was like, "Bullcrap! Yeah right."

So, here I was in a lot of pain, my drunken mom was yelling, and my BD was not there at all. Around 9 p.m. the doctors stated I had dilated to 5 centimeters, so the nurses gave me an epidural, and that made the pain a little better. But as they were giving me the shot in my back, it was very cold, and I could feel it going up my spine. It was getting late, and there was still no BD in sight. He had stopped answering his phone. I looked over at my drunk mother, and she had talked so much that she had fallen asleep from all the crap she was saying. But as I look back, she was right. She was right about everything. My nurse came in to move me to O/G triage where I had to deliver the baby. Man, I didn't want them to wake my mother up; heck, she had just gone to sleep from talking all that crap...stuff I didn't want to hear.

When they woke her, you could've sworn she was talking in her sleep because she awoke saying, "Shawn, this nigga doesn't love you or that motherfucking baby. You are just being stupid, and I'm not gonna take care of no damn baby."

After another 30 minutes of that, her husband came and picked her up.

Finally, I had peace and quiet and could try to sleep since I was very sleepy, but I couldn't. Around midnight, my BD came in high as heck, smelling like a pound of weed and not giving a care. I was so embarrassed because here we are about to have a baby and he comes up here high smelling like weed. **He didn't even ask how I was doing. He just asked about the baby, went over to the layout couch and went to sleep.**

I just started to cry, rubbing my stomach, and telling my son, "No matter what... I am always going to be here, and I will always take care of you the best way I can."

I thought about what the older lady had told me when I first found out I was pregnant with my son. She said to take care of my blessing, and I vowed that I would. I fell asleep and woke up around 3 a.m. the next morning. Troy woke up and said he was going to go to his aunt's house around the corner to change clothes and take a bath and that he would be right back. I was upset because I had dilated to 8 centimeters already, and he was risking not seeing our son's birth, but deep down, I knew he didn't give a care. He promised he was coming right back.

10:20 a.m. came, and I called.

Of course there was no answer, so I hung up and called again.

He picked up, but all I could hear was loud music and him saying, "I'm on my way in a minute, man."

So, I hung up the phone and started crying and thinking, *"Did I really keep this baby just to keep him around? Why didn't I just get an abortion?"*

I felt stupid, but it was too late to turn back now, and I wouldn't dream of giving my baby up for adoption. I quit thinking negatively because in a matter of minutes I was about to meet my baby boy, my child, and my blessing.

The doctor came and checked me, and it was time for me to push. I was scared and sad at the same time. I was sad because I was pushing my first child out at 18, but most of all, I was by myself and was scared because of the responsibilities I was about to have. The nurse came in to prepare me to push.

As they were laying my bed back, I was like, "Oh my gosh, this is real!"

This was about to happen. The doctor told me to push, so I did just that. I was pushing, and my head started hurting. I got dizzy all at once.

The doctor said, "Two more pushes Ms. Smith. Come on. One…" Before he could even get to two, I started pushing, and I started farting. It was loud like fire crackers. I was so embarrassed, but I kept pushing.

The doctor said, "Last one. Make it big!"

So, I held my breath, closed my eyes, and gave it all I had. I felt relief, as if I had held something in for a long time and it finally came out. My eyes were still closed, and I heard this sound—the most beautiful and precious sound I'd heard in my life, my son crying. As I opened my eyes, the doctor said, "Congratulations, Ms. Smith. It's a boy!"

They weighed him, wrapped him up, and gave him to me. He was so handsome and bright as his eyes opened. I started crying. I could not believe this little human being was inside of me, but most of all, he was my son and he belonged to me. As I looked in his eyes, it was like we had an instant connection.

I put my thumb in his fingers, and I held him close saying, "Mama is here son, and loves you so much."

He closed his eyes and opened them again as we made eye contact. My life changed. I saw hope in my son's eyes. I saw encouragement that I could do anything I put my mind to. I held my head high and looked out the window at the sky. I could not believe I was holding my very own child and that he came from my body. As I looked back at him, I realized that my life had just begun.

Both of our lives started together on Friday, November 10, 2006 at 11:13 a.m. The nurse came in and said they needed to clean him up and they would bring him back. I didn't want to let my baby go at all, but I had to. When they took him, I looked at my phone and saw that Troy had called. I called him back and told him he missed everything.

The only thing he could say was, "Damn. Smh, I told you I was right up the street."

I didn't want to go back and forth with him, so I just hung up and called my aunt Jessica, my mom, and my Grandad. My family got there quickly, and I told them where the baby was. I got in the wheelchair and my mom pushed me to the nursery. As I pulled up to the window, all the babies were covered up. The only thing you could see was their noses and eyes. I couldn't tell which one was my baby, but my Grandad could.

My Grandad said, "There he is! There is Mr. Bad-Ass," and he started smiling.

We were like, "How'd you know?"

He said, "Just know... I'm right. I know that is him."

The nurse came, looked at my wristband, and I kid you not, picked up the baby my Grandad said was my son. We all looked at him and laughed. My mom rolled me back to my room so I could get cleaned up. As she was rolling me into the room, my BD was sitting on the couch asking where the baby was.

My mom was pissed, and she started yelling at him, "You a sorry MF! If your butt was here, you would know."

She said, "Shawn, this nigga doesn't love you or that baby. You better leave his butt alone."

When my family saw he was there, they left, and the nurse brought the baby back to the room. Troy picked up our son, whose nickname was Trey.

As he was holding Trey, I thought to myself, *"Could this change him? Could he love us and me like he used to?"*

Two days went by, and it was time for us to be released from the hospital.

As I was holding Trey and being wheeled to the car, I couldn't help but think, *"Did I make a mistake by bringing a baby into this world? Am I going to be a good enough mother for my son?"*

When we made it home, I was so happy to have my son I made. Once we made it in the house, I laid Trey down and my BD watched him while I took a shower. When I got out of the shower, my Grandad said, "I will let that nigga stay the night to help you with this baby, but he can't move in here. I'm not taking care of no grown nigga, Shawn."

I told him, "I understand, Papa. Thank you for everything you are doing."

He kissed me on my forehead, and I walked back to the living room where Trey and Troy were. Troy asked me if I was hungry, and I told him I was. He went into the kitchen, cleaned up, and cooked. Man, when I tell you that man can cook, that man can cook his butt off! He cooked like those old school grannies that had that fat hanging from their arms. I dozed off with Trey lying on top of me.

When I woke up, he brought me a plate. We sat down and talked about what we were going to do. He told me he was ready to be in an actual relationship with me and that he was sorry for not being certain before. I forgave him because deep down, I really loved that man like I've never loved before. Troy had stayed around for the next couple of weeks because day by day, it was like I wasn't myself at all. I didn't know what was going on. When I went to the doctor, he had told me I was experiencing postpartum depression and that was normal. It didn't seem normal at all. When Trey would cry, he would cry so loudly. I couldn't take it at all. Sometimes, he would cry so loudly for so long.

You would have thought someone hurt him. It got to the point that I couldn't sleep. Trey was crying so badly that I broke down and started crying with him, wishing I didn't have to go through this. Maybe this was a sign that I should've listened, because I wasn't ready to have a baby at all.

It's like another person was coming out of me. I started crying and yelling, and Troy got out of the shower to ask what was wrong.

I told him I didn't want my baby anymore. Troy grabbed Trey from me and said, "You a liar, Shawn. What is wrong with you, and why are you saying that stupid crap?"

I shook my head and told him, "No, I'm not ready for this at all."

I just wanted to leave and never come back. I went into the bathroom and sat on the floor. I couldn't believe I said those things, but most of all, I couldn't believe I was going through this. Finally, Troy calmed Trey down after giving him a bath and a bottle and putting him to sleep. When I didn't hear any crying, it made me feel better. Troy knocked on the door asking if I was going to be okay. I just opened the door, and he came in and helped me off the floor.

He ran me a bath, put me in the tub and started bathing me and giving me a massage. He kissed me on my forehead and told me everything was going to be okay.

I told him I had gotten overwhelmed, and I felt like I wasn't doing a good job as a mom since Trey was crying like that. He told me babies cry all the time and that I needed to learn how to be patient with Trey, because he was just a baby. He kissed me again, helped me out the tub, and helped me get dressed. He stayed the night and held me all night. I missed that affection from him. He made sure I was able to get some rest that night. He got up throughout the night to get Trey and make sure he was fed and changed. The next day, he left and went back to his sister's house. My aunt came over to check on us,

I had started beating myself down and not being confident in myself anymore because I had gotten pregnant.

and she stayed over for a couple of days since she just had knee surgery. While she was there, she helped with Trey since it was time for me to go back to work and school. I had to enroll myself in night school at Trimble Tech and work on the weekends.

I met so many mothers at this school who were in the same position as me, so I felt more comfortable there.

On my first day, I met the principal, and it was the same principal I had at Dunbar High School. That made me even more comfortable. I was determined to graduate for myself, but mostly to make my Grandad proud. I had started beating myself down and not being confident in myself anymore because I had gotten pregnant (and could barely take care of myself and my child). The only thing that used to make me smile is when I remembered what my ROTC teacher used to tell me:

"Shawn, you are more than what your eyes see in that mirror. When you realize that, you will be able to conquer more in life. Until then, you will be the center of your self-pity party."

A couple of months went by, and it was almost time for the prom and graduation. My BD didn't want to go to my prom, so I went with my friends from school. I didn't know where to start when thinking about prom preparations and my Grandad didn't either.

He told me, "I will buy whatever you need, but Papa don't know nothing about no prom."

It was to the point that I was frustrated and didn't even want to go anymore, because nothing was working in my favor at all. I remember that I worked all Friday night and didn't get off until 5 p.m. the next day, and I still had to get ready for my prom. I had fixed my hair myself in a bun with some bangs and got dressed. My Grandad watched Trey and told me to go out and have a good time. He was going to make sure the baby was okay.

My Grandad drove me to the place where my prom was held and as I was getting out, I told him I had a way home.

He smiled and said, "Okay honey. You know, I'm here if you need me to come back."

He smiled, looked in the backseat and said, "Don't worry about me and Mr. 'Bad-Ass' (Trey's nickname he gave him). I'm about to go eat and go to sleep."

I gave my Grandad a hug and he said, "You are so beautiful, honey. Please have a good time." I promised him I would and got out of the car, and they drove off. When I walked in the building, my friends were waiting on me. I felt so beautiful that night and had so much fun. I hadn't had fun like that since I was like 14 years old. I felt so free, but most of all, I felt and looked good. I didn't stay until the prom was over because I started missing my baby. My friend took me home and when I got in, Trey and my Grandad were passed out and sleeping well. I got Trey and drew him a bath because I knew my Grandad didn't bathe him. His little neck smelled like stinky milk.

After we took our baths, we went to sleep. To be honest, I didn't care what anyone said since people think you can't live your life if you have a baby at an early age. I say they are wrong because I know that if I didn't have my son, I probably would not have pushed as hard and stayed focused to graduate on time.

The next morning, my Grandad cooked breakfast, and we sat down at the table and talked. He asked me if I was graduating, and I told him the state test results hadn't come back yet. He told me that no matter what, he was always going to be there.

"But your butt better graduate! Education is the key."

We both laughed. After I ate, I got ready for work and my Grandad dropped me off. My mom started pitching in to help me watch the baby while I worked and went to school. Until this day, I don't know why she started helping me with the baby.

Maybe it is because she felt sorry for me or she felt she was wrong for saying what she had said. I really don't know, but I appreciated her for helping.

On Monday, I got the state test results back, and I had failed.

They told us that if we didn't pass, we could still walk but we would not receive our diplomas until we passed. I cried my eyes out that day. I was so hurt that I didn't pass the test. Yes, I was going to walk, but it was going to be fake because I didn't earn it like I should have. I felt like a failure. I felt like the stupid person my mom always said I was. As I prepared for my graduation, I felt bad for pretending that I was going to receive my high school diploma, but I had no choice. I didn't want my Grandad to not

I felt like a failure. I felt like the stupid person my mom always said I was.

be proud of me. Besides, I'd worked hard and received all my credits and more. The only thing I was missing was passing the state test. So, I made sure I was enrolled in summer school to take the test again. I didn't tell hardly anyone about my graduation because I only had my Grandad, mom, aunt and a few friends and family. As we came from the back and sat down by our names, I looked over but couldn't find my Grandad or my son. If no one else showed up, I knew those two were there for sure.

Our 2007 graduating class was not big, but it was big enough to pack the auditorium with love and support. As we lined up by the stage and they called my name, I looked in the front of the audience and my Grandad and son were standing there. My Grandad was standing proud while crying and clapping. Trey was in his arms, and he made sure my son saw me walk across that stage. It made me cry as I was walking across because I was so proud of myself, but most of all, I didn't look like a failure to the two most important people in my life.

As I shook my principal's hands, she told me, "I'm so proud of you, young lady. You did it."

I smiled, gave her a hug, got the rolled-up paper and sat down. I just couldn't stop crying and looking at my son because if it wasn't for him, I don't know if I would have made it this far in life. I wanted to show him that nothing can hold you back. You can achieve anything you put your mind to. When we stood up as a class and threw up our caps, a warm spirit seemed like it had wrapped around me. I got so warm inside. I really can't explain the feeling. As we all walked outside to our families, some of us walked out to nice cars, but I walked out to the love and support. I was so happy to see my Grandad and son standing there waiting for me.

My Grandad was just smiling, and he was tearing up. I'd never seen my Grandad cry, but

I did that day.

He said, "I'm so proud of you, honey. You kept your word, and you did it. You didn't let Papa down."

As we got in the car, Trey was sound asleep, and my Grandad took us home and made some homemade burgers and fries. Man, I loved his homemade hamburgers; they were the best.

As we sat down and he brought my plate to me, he asked, "What are your plans in life?"

I looked and said, "I really haven't thought about it."

I just wanted to stay with my Grandad, work, and take care of Trey.

He said, "Little girl, Papa's not always gonna be here. You need to think of something."

We laughed and talked some more. Then he went in his room and went to sleep. I stayed up that night studying for the state test. I'd become so determined to pass that test that I didn't want anything to get in my way, so I focused. I went to summer school, worked, and studied my butt off.

I was not nervous on the day of the test. I was very confident that I had put in the work to pass, and I was going to receive a positive outcome. I took the test and the results came back within a couple of weeks. The day the results came in, I was nervous to open the letter. When I opened it up and saw that I had not only passed, but also made one of the top scores in FWISD. Man, I was so shocked! I really did *that* well.

I had received my high school diploma, and I was okay from there. Until this day, I never told anyone that I failed the first time. I will take that to my grave.

After school was completed, I picked up a second job at Home Depot that paid $10 per hour. Those paychecks were good at that time because I was able to provide for my son and help my Grandad with the rent. After speaking with a couple of my friends and seeing they had no plans, I decided I was going to do a nursing program.

But I didn't know where to start.

One day after work, a commercial came on about getting a medical billing and coding license. I went for it. I enrolled myself in the nine-month program. During this time, I still had my Grandad and my family's full support. However, I was mad because Troy was living life and left me with all the responsibilities of Trey. At the same time, I started missing him. Yes, I had my family's support, but while going through the ups and downs with Troy, I learned that my son and Grandad couldn't give me the type of companionship that he could. I stayed focused, graduated, and decided I wanted to move out because my Grandad was getting old. I felt he needed his own space. Besides, I wanted to try the "family thing" with Troy when he came back from college.

Chapter 2
THE PAIN

As I look back, I should have just stayed with my Grandad to avoid all the crap I was about to encounter in life. It seems like everything I was taught went out the window because I was blinded by love.

But one thing I never learned is that love doesn't hurt. I had to learn that the hard way.

Just to lend some advice, when you have older people telling you things about life, *listen*. They have already been there and done that. They are trying to help you avoid going through what they went through.

I remember my Grandad's twin sister told me, "Little girl, don't be like me. Don't fall for the first nigga you get. Explore life, but most of all, *enjoy* life. But I can tell you're not going to listen to what I'm telling you, and that nigga you get with is going to put your life through hell."

I just looked and told her, "Thanks for the advice."

By this time, I had graduated and moved into my own apartment with Troy. Everything was perfect at first. He was starting to be the man I wanted him to be. I got a job at JPS hospital in medical records and was making good money. I got a brand new car, so it seemed like life was going in the right direction…until I had let one of my friends stay with me until she got on her feet.

I noticed that Troy was starting to change. He started staying out all night. I was letting things go that I should have been addressing. One day, my friend and her boyfriend were arguing. I really didn't want to get into that because it wasn't my business, so I stayed in my room.

But Troy was like, "We don't do that crap over here. Not with my son in here sleeping."

So, he got up and went into the living room. He came back saying that my friend's boyfriend beat her up, took her money and left.

I sat there for a minute and Troy said, "Let me go see if I can go find this nigga so she won't call the police and get us in trouble."

I was like, "Okay, baby. Be safe."

He left, and I went into the living room to check on my friend. When I saw her face, I wanted to cry. He had beaten her up so badly that she didn't even want to look me in my eyes. By this time, I didn't care about her calling the police because no man should put their hands on a woman. I asked her if she was okay.

She said, "Yes, I'm fine. He just got mad that I didn't want to give him some money to buy him some weed. So, he beat me up."

I asked her, "Is this normal?"

She said, "Almost..."

I looked, and I didn't understand how she could allow him to treat her this way. So, I told her I didn't need that around my child.

She said, "We will be leaving next week. Can we stay until then?"

I looked and said, "So... you want that nigga to stay too, huh?"

She said, "Please, Shawn. We don't have anywhere to go, but I promise we will be out of here next week."

I said, "But I can't have this crap around my son."

She said, "I understand. From now on, I just have to do what he says and not make him mad."

I said, "Okay, man…" and walked into my room.

I wasn't mad at her, but I was very disappointed in her because she worked her butt off every day and she was allowing him to do this to her. I didn't know how she felt due to the fact that Troy never put his hands on me. Yes, we would argue, but it never got to the point to where he would put his hands on me. I wanted to try to understand why she was allowing this to happen, but I couldn't.

But to be honest, I wasn't any better than her because I worked my butt off, and Troy didn't have a job either. The only difference was I wasn't getting abused, but I was stupid for not knowing my worth at the time.

So, as I was making my way back to my room, I turned around and told her, "When you get tired, you will leave."

She smiled and said, "You're right."

Troy came home around 2 a.m., and I was

pissed because he hadn't done that in a long time. I was worried because he didn't call to let me know he was okay. On top of that, I had to be at work at 7 a.m. But me being stupid, I didn't say anything. I just went back to sleep when he walked through the door.

That morning in the car on my way to work, I was silent, and he asked what was wrong. I didn't say anything. When we pulled up to my job, I gave Trey a kiss and told him I loved him. I just looked at Troy like he was a pile of crap and walked into the building.

Over the next couple of days, I noticed I was happy at work, but when it was time to leave, I didn't even want to go home. Troy started picking me up late, and we started arguing more. I could feel the change in our relationship, which should have been a red flag to leave. But, I stayed. We started being disrespectful toward one another. He started being impatient with our son, staying out late, and making me late to work daily. However, I didn't let that get me down because I had gotten a promotion at work with better pay, better hours, and my own office right beside the Director of Nursing in the surgery department. I had gotten so close to the Director of Nursing that I started telling her about my problems at home. She was a very positive person, but she was also honest with me.

She told me, "Watch how he reacts when you tell him about your promotion. If he is excited as much as you are, the love is still there. You all just need better communication skills, and you need to help him find a job because at the end of the day, he is a man and a father. He needs to be the sole provider, not you. But if he is not as excited as you, he is just keeping you around for beneficial reasons, and it is time for you all to part ways before the hatred gets worse."

So that day when I got off work, I was happy and all smiles. When I got in the car, I had told him about the promotion. He was not as excited as me, but he showed a little excitement, I guess. When he showed that crap, I realized everything she said was true, and it was time for us to end the relationship before it went downhill from there.

He dropped us off at home. I left a text on his phone telling him that he needed to take into consideration that I got this new position, and I needed to be at work on time from here on out. Since I was paying all the bills and making sure we were good, I never nagged him for not being able to do that, but we would have to work together as a team if we were going to try to make this work.

He texted back some slick crap that I really can't remember. But I do remember that he came home at 4 a.m. that morning. I bet he thought I wasn't going to say anything.

Wrong! He had me messed up at this point. When I heard those keys opening up that dang door, I jumped up out that bed like a black ninja.

I was like, "Where the hell have you been? It's 4 in the morning, and I have to be at work at 7 a.m. I texted and told you that."

My friend and her boyfriend were still living there. I didn't give a care. I just went on a rant.

I said, "You act like you pay these bills and put gas in that car. Newsflash! I do all that crap, my nigga, so we need to work together to make sure I get to work on time."

By this time, my friend and her boyfriend had woken up and my friend was asking if everything was okay.

I said, "Yeah, it's fine."

Her boyfriend started laughing and looking at my BD. He said, "My nigga, I told you that you need to start controlling her. You let her treat you like a hoe."

I looked at him and said, "Nigga! You can get out of my house." By this time, my BD had started calling me disrespectful names. No matter what the argument was before, he had never called me those names. I turned and just walked away toward my room, and my BD grabbed me by my hair and pushed me to the ground. He got on top of me and started hitting me in my face and calling me names. He had hit me so hard that I started seeing stars in my head. I thought he was going to kill me. The way he was hitting me seemed as if he couldn't wait to whoop my butt. I tried to get up and run, and he picked me up and body slammed me. I hit my head so hard on the carpet. He had started dragging me into the room by my hair, and Trey had woken up, crying and trying to get to me. He started yelling at Trey.

"Who was going to take care of Trey if he killed me? Will he kill my son too?"

I told him, "Don't be yelling at him! He is just a baby." When I said that, he hit me in my mouth so hard that I started bleeding and spitting out blood. He dragged me into the closet and put a wire hanger around my neck. I could barely breathe.

He said, "Is this what you want, bitch? Do you want to die, bitch? I will kill your bitch ass right now!"

I didn't say anything. The only thing I could think about was, "Who was going to take care of Trey if he killed me? Or will he kill my son too?"

Since I wasn't saying anything, he got even madder and hit me so hard in my head that I had blacked out. Until this day, I don't know how long I was out.

But when I woke up, I saw Trey sitting by me in his diaper, crying while rubbing my head and saying, "Mama."

His eyes were so red and swollen from crying. I didn't know what to do. I tried to get up, but my body and head were in so much pain, so I lay there for a couple minutes. When I regained my energy, I got up.

Now I'm going to pause right there and let you parents know that until this day, I struggled with my son and his anger management problems. He is 10-years-old now, and he remembers everything that happened that night. He doesn't want me talking to other men because he feels he must always protect me. He has nightmares of his daddy hitting me and him and killing us. Even though this happened when he was little, it messed up his mind and he rarely trusts anyone. His anger issues are so bad that sometimes I can't control them.

If you find yourself in this situation, please leave for the sake of your children because this is going to stick with them for the rest of their lives. At this point, I must send him to therapy, and that is the consequence of my staying and allowing him to see me being treated that way. No child should see their mother or father being abused in any form, shape, or fashion. They deserve to live a care-free life. Remember, don't wait until it's too late to come up with a game plan and leave. Your child's life depends on it.

Now, back to the story!

I grabbed him, and I felt his little heart beating like it was about to give out. He was sweating, shaking, and his eyes were so red and puffy from crying.

All I could say was, "I'm sorry. Daddy was

just angry. He didn't mean to do it."

If I had known what I know now, I would have called the police and left. But I stayed. I stayed thinking that it was never going to happen again. I stayed blaming myself for making him so angry that he took it that far. From that point on, I watched how I spoke to him because I wanted to keep him happy, not knowing I was degrading myself in front of my son.

Chapter 3
TWO BLACK EYES

They say you can't help who you love. Currently in my life, the only unconditional love I was receiving was coming from my son. I did not know that love doesn't hurt, and love is not painful.

When a person loves you, they don't hurt themselves or the people around them.

At this stage of our relationship, I was still determined not be a statistic.

I could remember the day I found out I was pregnant with Trey and the hateful things my mother said. I started thinking maybe she was right. Maybe I took the wrong path because I didn't listen and tried to do the right thing by not aborting my baby.

Was she right?

I asked myself that every day.

So, we moved to another apartment, and I thought we were going to be okay. Boy, was I wrong. It had gotten worse. We were arguing every day and being disrespectful toward each other, but I still loved him as if we had just met.

My heart wanted to stay, but my mind was ready to leave. I honestly felt that my mind had shut down on me for a minute because of the things I was allowing to happen—the disrespect and the abuse. Even though I was going through that, I kept a smile every day because I felt in my heart and soul that one day everything was going to be okay.

I never had a bad heart. I wasn't raised or taught to have one.

I used to see my mom get misused and go back. I used to see the women I was around get physically, emotionally, and mentally abused, but they never gave up. Is that why I stayed? I still can't answer that question, to be honest. I remember one day, after Troy had stayed out all night when I had to be at work, I had gotten so afraid that I stopped taking up for myself. So, he came in asking for some money, and I told him we had to pay the rent and buy food, so I didn't have it. Trey was in the living room watching TV and eating his cereal.

He had grown so accustomed to the arguing and fighting that it didn't even faze him anymore. On this day, (I remember it like it was yesterday) my BD had come in needing money that I just didn't have.

After I told him I didn't have it, I saw this look on his face and his eyes were so black that in my heart, I said, "Just give it to him, so he won't hurt you. Give it to him to make him happy so he can just leave."

Normally, I would listen to my heart, but on this day, it's like my mind kicked in and said, *"No! Don't give it to him. You are responsible for giving your son a roof over his head and taking care of him. If you give it away, who is going to take care of the bills?"*

His eyes were black, but my heart was so pure, and I knew it was time. My pure heart had gotten me nowhere. I created this monster, a man who I didn't make see his full potential or live up to the role that my Granddad had filled all those years. When said I didn't have it, he pushed me and grabbed my purse to take the money.

I grabbed my purse back, crying, telling him, "No, Troy! You can't take our money. We need this money. Where are we going to stay? How are we going to eat?"

He pushed me so hard onto the bed and closed the door. He started hitting me in my face, stomach, and everywhere he could to hurt me. He ripped off my panties and forced himself on me. I felt so disgusted that I thought I was going to throw up. I couldn't believe this was happening, and I pushed him off of me and hit the window, trying to get out. Blood and glass was everywhere, and I had cut myself. He grabbed me again, and at that moment, I thought he was going to kill me. *He didn't care where or how hard he was hitting me, and I knew he was aiming to kill me.* As I lay on the floor, I saw the shadow of little feet at the door as if my son was listening. I tried to get to the door, but he started choking me and put a pillow over my face. From that moment, I knew I was going to die, and the last thing I was going to see was those little feet.

I yelled out, "Just take the money and go!

Please, I can't breathe!"

He rose up, and I ran toward the door, opened it and saw Trey balled up in a corner. I knew this man was going to kill me so I ran to the front door, and as I ran, he grabbed me by my hair and pulled me back. I saw drops of blood, but I learned at that moment I was tired of getting my butt whooped. One of us was not going to make it out alive. As he pulled me back, I grabbed a glass vase, hit him in the head and ran out the door. I didn't have anything but a bloody t-shirt on, but I didn't care. I wanted to live. I ran to Ms. Coreen's house and knocked on her door.

She came to the door and said, "What the hell is going on? What happened to you?"

I fell on her front steps and told her, "Please call 911! He trying to kill me."

Right when I said that I saw him running, holding his head with blood all on his shirt. I got up and ran but didn't know where I was going. I was trying to get away, but my legs gave out and I fell. He grabbed my head and started hitting my face like I was nothing to him, like he never loved me. I've never in my life felt pain like when he was hitting me then. I just kept my eyes closed and tried to block the punches. There I was in the middle of the concrete, naked and getting the crap beaten out of me. I heard the police sirens, and he stopped hitting me and ran. He had run and He jumped in my car and took off. I crawled to the grass and just lay there. I couldn't see out of the eyes. The only thing I saw was blood, and I wanted to die. The paramedic picked me up and put me on the stretcher and asked me for my name.

I started yelling, "My son, my son! He is in the house balled up in a corner. Please make sure he didn't take my son."

The police asked, "Ma'am, what is your apartment number?" When he asked that, I blacked out due to losing so much blood.

I don't know how and when my mom came and got my son, but she had him when I woke up at JPS hospital in the surgery department. When I woke up, my vison in my left eye was very blurred, but I could still see out of my right, and I had a cast on my right arm.

I looked around, and all I saw was Trey sleeping in my godsister's arms in the same clothes with no shoes on.

My godsister laid him down and came over to ask if I was okay. I shook my head yes. She said Mama (my godmother) said Trey and I could move in with them until I got on my feet again. I just lay there in my own self-pity. She took Trey home with her, and I tried to get some sleep. When I woke up, the phone was ringing, and the nurse gave me the phone.

I said, "Hello," and it was him.

He said, "I'm sorry that this happened. Your car is outside in the front," and hung up the phone.

I started crying because I was relieved and alive. I told the policeman where my car was, but I didn't tell him he was the one who had called. They parked the car and brought my keys. I stayed in the hospital for a week. I had minor brain damage but my vision in my left eye was permanently damaged. When I was released, Trey and I went and stayed with my godmother and my godsister in a two-bed-room apartment. We slept on the couch. They helped me get him enrolled in school and bought his school clothes and supplies. My godsister and I were on the hunt for jobs every day. My godmother never showed any signs that she wanted us to leave, but I felt we were being a burden on her. I got back into church, and God blessed me with a job that

I didn't have any experience in. I got my first call center job at Bank of America. The day I started is the day Troy was taken to jail. Of course, I was the one accused of telling the police his location. He went to jail, and I felt I had to be there for him. Maybe he would change. They gave him one month in jail. I started communicating with his Mama again and left my godmother's apartment because I didn't want to worry her anymore.

As I look back now, I see how very selfish and unappreciative that was.

I moved in with Troy's Mama and her husband, and they helped us out a lot. They bought us new clothes, gave us a place to stay, and made sure everything was okay every day.

Mind you, only my mom knew what happened. My other family members didn't know what was going on. I used to visit my Grandad, and I knew he had a feeling something was not right; He just couldn't pin the nail on it. So, I stayed at his mom's house and worked. While working at the bank, I got to meet up with an old friend from school who then became one of my best friends. I got to meet some very nice people who became my work family. I always went to work with a smile on my face. I felt so free, so great. I never had been that free before. My Bank of America family would always go to Applebee's on Thursdays and drink, talk about life issues, laugh, and have a really good time.

How I miss those days!

But those days helped me grow and to trust people and share my problems.

They were truly a family. During this time, my mother went to prison. I had a relationship with my mother, but then again, I didn't. As I stayed with Troy's mother she helped me grow a little. She gave me a lot of insight on her relationship with Troy's father. I should have known that the apple doesn't fall too far from the tree. I started writing him again and visiting him in prison.

Now at the time, I didn't see it as a set-up but as I look back I saw that the reason his mom stepped in to help us was so I could take him back.

My family tells me it was because she didn't want him to be dependent on her, but I'm not sure. Whatever it was, it worked.

She told me to dress up in lingerie when he came home and to love him no matter what. In January 2011, I moved to some apartment in Woodhaven just before he was released, and I wanted everything to be as perfect as if it was when we first moved in together. Little did I know, our relationship would never be perfect, and it sure wasn't going to be like it was in the beginning. They say there are always little signs, but we never pay attention to them.

When he was released, his mom threw him a welcome home party. I remember riding with his mom to pick him up from prison in Mineral Wells. I was so anxious and happy to see him. As he walked out, I was happy; jumping up and down and crying, not knowing he was about to do the same things in only a matter of time. After he was released, we got back together and went home, and I did actually what his mom said to do. I dressed in some purple lingerie with some purple heels, my long hair hanging to my butt. I turned on some slow music and started dancing for him, kissing him, and grabbing on him. He was just smiling from ear to ear. I grabbed his hand and walked him to the bedroom, and we got it on like Marvin Gaye.

He was very helpful and active in the beginning. I introduced him to my best friend at the time. He was looking for a job, cooking, cleaning, and helping with Trey. He was doing great in the beginning, and I found out I was pregnant with my first little girl. He was very excited. Now mind you, he had already had a little girl older than Trey. As I got farther along in my pregnancy, my best friend started coming over a lot. She and Troy started hanging out more. I never thought they would mess around or anything of that nature because she was in a relationship. I feel making them too comfortable around each other was where I went wrong. She was like the best friend I never had—always there, always positive, always helping me no matter the situation. Anyway, my coworkers threw me a baby shower. We had a good time that day.

But the problems started arising at home.

Troy had gone back to hanging out, not coming home, not looking for a job, and spending less time with Trey. This go around, I always called him out on his crap, and he didn't like that. So, the arguing and fighting started back up. I went on maternity leave from my job; therefore, I was at home more. He was always gone always with his homeboys—going to the club, and I started getting jealous because I felt that he should be at home with his family instead of being gone all day in my car—a car I had to fill up with gas and pay to maintain and insure.

Around this time, my mother got out of jail, and my Grandad had made plans for her to stay with him until she had gotten back on her feet. She left with my stepdad like she always did and hurt my Grandad's feelings, even though he didn't show it. Again, my Grandad was my backbone. He was always there to help me no matter what, but he was getting tired of all the fighting that was going on in my relationship, so he started to keep his distance. Jealousy as well as hate was formed in my relationship. I wanted to leave but I knew I would have to fight to do so; besides, I wanted Trey to have both parents around even if it was hurting me.

On December 18, 2011, I had my baby girl. She was 10 lbs, 5 oz, and I remember saying how big she was when she was born. At first, she wasn't crying, and they kept spanking her but she wouldn't respond. They had to rush her to the NICU because her sugar levels had dropped. I started panicking and crying because I thought something was going to happen to my baby. She had to stay a week after I was discharged. Troy and I both were up there every day with her. He loved her to death— that was his baby girl. The way he used to gaze in her eyes every day from the doctor's visits and at home, I knew we were going to be alright. However, when she was two or three months old, we *Jealousy as well as hate was formed in my relationship. I wanted to leave but I knew I would have to fight to do so.* were back to the fighting and arguing. This time, I was trying to leave. So, we fought, and he took my keys and left. I kept calling him to come and get the kids because I needed a break. I didn't feel like myself, and I didn't want to be around my kids like that. I texted and told him I was going to leave the kids by themselves if he didn't come back. My doctor said I was going through postpartum depression, but at that time, I didn't know what was going on. All I knew was I was not myself, and I needed to leave. I walked out the door and sat on the staircase. I texted him again and said I was gone and that the kids were alone. I told him he needed to come get them, and I waited until I saw the car pull in. He got out and walked in the door. He ran back outside looking around for me, and then he called his mother. As he was telling his mother that I abandoned the kids, I just started walking. I didn't have shoes on and didn't know where I was going, but I couldn't figure out what was wrong with me. I walked from my house to my mother's apartment on my bare feet, looking all kinds of crazy.

When I showed up and knocked on the door, my stepdad was more concerned than my mom.

She just said she didn't want the drama at her house. I told my stepdad what happened, and I stayed at their house that night. The next day, I called Troy to check on the kids, and he told me that his mother had called Child Protective Services (CPS). He said I wasn't going to get them back since I had abandoned them. I called my aunt and cousins to go with me back to the apartment so I could get some things.

When I got to my apartment, all my things were gone, even my clothes.

I called his mother, and she said that her son wanted to take the things out the apartment because he didn't know if I was coming back or not. I asked if she could bring me my things and she refused, which pissed me off. So, I called the police and reported my things stolen. They only made a report.

A week had gone by, and I had to find another apartment. That was the only way I could get my kids and my things. We had a meeting with CPS, and I had to find someone to get temporary custody of my kids. The CPS lady didn't even give me a chance. Both of my aunts were willing to get my kids, but until this day I think Troy's mom lied about my family so that temporary custody was given to her. I was crying, begging, and telling them that I didn't leave them alone, but it was his mother's word against mine. Troy had also given the CPS the texts I had sent to him, so that didn't make it any better. I moved to the Brentwood apartment, and by this time, I had CPS in my life, and my children were in temporary custody of Troy's mother. I had to take some anger management classes and drug tests to get them back.

I got up swinging because I was at the point where I was tired of all this drama. I didn't want to go through it anymore. *Why Shawn? Why did you go back?* I picked up my phone to call the police, and Troy grabbed my phone and ran out the door. Trey and the girls were in the next room with the door closed. The bad thing about it is that Trey had gotten so used to us fighting that it didn't faze him anymore. He just made sure his sisters were out of the way and safe. I went to my downstairs neighbor's house and called the police. The police arrived and it was the same black cop from the incident in the other apartment. I didn't remember him, but he remembered me.

He said, "So you actually went back after how he beat you up the last time?"

I couldn't do anything but look down. He pulled me away from the other cop, and we started walking.

He said, "My daughter was 21 when she was beaten to death by her husband. I don't want to be having a coroner come and get your body because you don't value yourself or those kids. This man doesn't love you, and he never will, so you need to leave. If you can't leave right off, make a plan and stick to it. Leave, please, before you end up dead."

He had tears in his eyes, and I could tell he was serious. The other officer walked up and asked for my license plate and the type of clothes Troy had on. I gave him the information, and they gave me a report.

The cop gave me his personal number and said, "Please consider what I said before it's too late. All it takes is one hit to the head, and you're gone. Please, Ms. Farr, get those kids and leave."

I walked back into the house, went to the bathroom and looked at myself in the mirror. I started crying.

Why me?

Then this voice said, *"Do it, then. Kill yourself."*

I looked in the mirror, and I was done. I really told myself that I wanted to die. I found some Tylenol PM, got a glass of water, and decided I was going to kill myself. I popped open the bottle and poured all the pills in my mouth. As I grabbed for the glass of water, a cold feeling came over my body as if someone was hugging me. As that cold feeling was wrapping around my body, I heard a cry—it was the crying of all my kids mixed into one. I spit all the pills in the sink and ran into the room where my kids were.

They were sound asleep, and no one was crying. Until this day, I can hear that crying sound when I want to give up on something, and it keeps me going in life no matter how rough things get. I cleaned up the house and took a shower. I prayed hard for trying to kill myself. I went to sleep in the kids' room with Trey on one arm, Renee on the other, and Lashay on top of my chest. I needed to feel them around me for me to sleep well.

The next morning when I woke up, the lights were off, and I didn't have the money to pay the light bill. I called Troy from my neighbor's phone, and he came and got us and took us over to his sister's house. On the way over, he kept apologizing and promised it wouldn't happen again. I told him that if he ever put his hands on me again I would leave and not come back. We stayed with his sister for a couple of weeks.

While we were living there, he proposed to me, and I thought he was really a changed man.

Around my birthday on July 4th, one of my friends took me out for my birthday. I was so happy to go and also to be kid-free. Troy and

I argued before I left, and he told me to be sure I came home that night. Well, we went out and had a good time, but we were drunk and barely made it to her house afterward. Her boyfriend had to drive us home, and she let me sleep on the couch and told me she would get me home bright and early.

The next day, I jumped up and it was already bright outside, and everyone was still sleeping. I looked at my phone, and I had missed calls and text messages from Troy. I was scared that he was going to beat me. I woke up my friend, and she and her boyfriend took me home. When I pulled up in front of the house, Troy was sitting on the porch mad as hell.

My friend asked, "Shawn, are you going to be okay? I'm scared for your safety."

I said, "I will be okay. I will call you if I need you."

Right as I hit the porch, he started saying I was out all night cheating on him. We argued that whole day, and then he left. His sister had cooked and fed the kids, and we went to sleep in my niece's room.

The next morning, I got up, took a bath, and saw I had a missed call from my friend.

I went outside to call her since everyone was still sleep. I told her I was okay, and she made a joke and started laughing. Then, Troy came up and accused me of talking about him. I told her I was going to call her back. I was laughing because I wasn't even thinking about him, so he grabbed my phone and threw it. I knew that look in his eye meant he was going to beat me up, so I ran to the door and told them to call the police.

He grabbed me by my hair and said, "So, you think you gon' be messing with another man now?"

I kept saying that I got drunk and went to sleep, and by this time, one of his nephews had given me a phone. I called the police, and he slapped the phone out of my hand and pushed me down.

I told him, "If you hit me, I'm leaving, and I'm not coming back. And I mean that."

As I was getting up, he pushed me back down to the ground.

His oldest nephew kept saying, "Come on, uncle. Don't do it, please."

He pushed him out of the way and came for me again. As I tried to stand up and swing, he body-slammed me on the ground. As soon as he got on top of me, the police were coming up the street, so he ran. Man, I was happy to see that police car. The other cop cars that were following Troy turned their sirens on to go chase him down. I talked to the police and called my grandad to come get me and the kids and my stuff. He came, and we went to his house. I told him he could take me home because the lights had come on that morning.

He said, "Shawn, if I take you to your apartment, he is going to try to kill you and these kids. Open your eyes, little girl, there is no next time. That damn fool is gonna kill you."

When we made it to his house, he sat me down and said I could stay as long as I wanted. I thanked him, and he kissed me on my forehead. We stayed with my grandad a couple of days, and then I told him to take me to the apartment to get some clothes since we were running out.

When I got to the apartment, all my stuff was gone and it was just a mess. My downstairs neighbor told me he sold all our things. I just started crying, which my Grandad hated.

He kept saying, "Honey, don't cry. I'm here with you and these kids. I will help no matter what."

He also told me that he didn't want to bury me, so if I went back to Troy, he would never speak to me again. I had no choice but to leave, because I couldn't risk our relationship.

Chapter 4
Pure-Hearted

I was blessed and grateful that she let me in just like that. Even though these apartments were in the ghetto, I didn't care as long as my kids had a roof over their heads. As you can see, things were going in my favor. I got a high-paying job and an apartment without having to depend on my grandad. I was proud of myself, and I never knew how strong I could be until I got through my past experiences and started achieving again.

I got a call one day from my brother telling me that our mom was very sick and that she was living in a rundown motel.

He also told me that I needed to go get her. At the time, I didn't mind going to get her because she needed me, and I needed her. My mother didn't fully raise me, so I never experienced that full mother's love.

Growing up, I was always at someone else's house whether it was an auntie's or a close friend's. I will never knock her for not taking care of me to the fullest, but I always wondered why she didn't take care of me like she did my little sister. My Grandad played the biggest part in raising me. As I got older, my aunt Sheila looked after me as well. Until this day, she treated me like I was one of hers. My aunt Sheila was the life of the party. Even though she was always drunk, she was one of the people in my life who would always be honest with me whether I liked it or not. I needed that from time to time, because I was hardheaded and sometimes I needed to have my feelings hurt in order to listen.

So, I went and got my mother, and she moved in with me and the kids. She watched my youngest a lot while I worked. Sometimes, I didn't get to see my babies for days because I was working so much, but my mom filled in for me. I had to work so that my mom didn't have to. As long as she was taking care of her health and helping with the kids, we were going to be okay. By this time, I had gotten a car, so I didn't have to hitch rides back and forth to work. I would go visit my grandad from time to time, but I had gotten so busy with work that I was forgetting to spend time with my kids and grandad.

I remember the Christmas of 2013, we had a get-together at my brother's house. We were laughing, talking, and having a really good time. Grandad started talking about death, and everyone was still joking and laughing.

I remember telling him, "Grandad, if you die, I will jump in that casket with you. I can't live without you."

He said, "No, you will have to continue to live your life. I've lived mine, honey," and he kissed me on my forehead.

We all went back to talking, laughing, and having a good time. I still didn't slow down and spend time with my loved ones. I was still on the go at work, and although I was making money, I wasn't showing my loved ones any type of love. I thought making money was enough, but it wasn't. On February 17, I went to my grandad to give him his money back, and he didn't want to take it. I saw a wet stain on his pants, but I didn't want to say anything to hurt his feelings. I asked him if he was okay, and he told me everything was fine. He smiled and gave me a kiss on my forehead, and I left. On February 23, I went back over to his house, and we sat and talked for a long time.

He had cooked some navy beans, so I ate and he played with the kids. As I was walking to the car, I noticed his skin was darker. He put the kids in their car seats, made sure they were buckled up, and stood at the car. I was on social media and didn't even notice him standing there just looking at me and smiling.

I looked over and told him I loved him.

He said he loved me too and gave me a kiss on my forehead.

If I would have known that was going to be the last time I saw him, I would have stayed or spent more time with him. On February 26, I was getting calls from an unknown number. I got off work at 8:00, and at 8:26 p.m., I was driving home when my mother called.

She said, *"Shawn, I'm so sorry to tell you, but your grandad was found dead. He's gone, baby."* I ran a red light and almost had a wreck trying to go pick them up just to go to his house. I couldn't believe it. I had just saw him three days before, and he was fine. But as I look back, he was sick and was showing signs of his liver failing. We didn't even know because he always kept things like that from us. As I pulled to the front of his apartment, the police were there. I just got out of the car and ran to his door. Before I could open the door, the police came out and grabbed me.

I broke down crying, saying, "No, not my grandad! Please tell me it's not true. Grandad, please don't leave me. I can't live without you!"

As I fell to the ground, you would have thought I was shot. My mind was not functioning at all, and I couldn't wrap my mind around being here on this Earth without my grandad. My mom came and grabbed me and walked me downstairs.

When I got there, my aunt Sheila was there. We had to go downstairs until the ambulance came and pronounced him dead. Shortly after, the corner came, and we had to go in and identify him. My aunt J, my brother, my mom, Trey, my aunt Sheila, and I were in the living room. They had to cover him up because he didn't have any clothes on. They dressed him, put him in the coroner bag, and brought him to the living room. As they were unzipping the bag, I was praying it wasn't him, but it was just my mind playing tricks on me. As they opened that bag and I saw him lying there lifeless, I looked over to my son Trey who bursted out crying and started trying to get to him.

He kept saying, "Papa, please get up. It's Trey. Please get up."

I had to pick up my son up and take him out of there. We went outside, and the coroner loaded up my Grandad's body in the van and left.

I remember my Grandad used to always say, "When I'm gone, my spirit will leave this body, and at the end of the day, it will just be a body. Don't cry because I've lived my life. You still must live yours, honey."

As I looked back on all the time we had together, he always tried to prepare us for the time when we had to live without him. I never knew how strong I was until I had to live without my backbone, Mr. Billy Ray Farr Sr. I can honestly say he kept his word to my grandmother and raised me to the best of his ability. When he saw we were going to be okay without him, my Granny came back and got him. Those next couple of days,

I didn't eat or sleep or leave my bedroom. My aunt J stepped up and took care of everything, from his final resting clothes to his funeral to cleaning out his apartment. Unto this day, I don't know how she did it.

The day he was found dead, both she and my brother called me to tell me that they had found him, but they couldn't get to me until I got off work. With her stepping up, we started to form a relationship. She stayed over at my house until the wake and the funeral.

Seeing him in that casket, I thought he looked as if he was resting peacefully. It really looked like he was sleeping.

His skin was bright and clear, his hair was a shiny, cold, black color, and he didn't need any makeup on him at all. The day of his funeral, my aunt Sheila was drunk as a skunk but she was always there no matter what. I spoke and read a poem, and got to see family members I haven't seen since we were little. I watched my mom say her goodbyes with my kids around her. It didn't hit me until my aunt walked up there and bent down to kiss him, and she let out this cry; a cry of pain.

I went up there with her, and she kissed him and told him she was so proud of him. She finally stood up, and we walked back, and then it was my brother's turn. My brother D was my grandad's world. When my uncle was killed, my big brother filled that space for my grandad. As my brother was up there, he was crying but he didn't break down as I expected him to. Unto this day, I know the death of my grandad hurts him every day, but he tries to stay strong for his little family and us. As they were carrying my grandad to the car, every second was surreal. I couldn't believe I was not going to see my grandad ever again.

How do you live without seeing someone who you've seen almost every day for 26 years?

As we got to the burial site, they took him out and placed him in the center up front. The two army men pulled his flag off his casket and folded it a certain way and placed his purple heart in it and handed the flag to my mother, but she then handed the flag to my aunt J. I will never forget as I took my last breath around him, I could feel him standing nearby, just smiling. As they rolled him to where he would be buried forever, I just stopped and looked at the casket. I just wanted a sign that he crossed over happily. I blew a kiss and left. That night I had a dream I was standing in this strange room, and he walked over to me.

I asked, "Why Papa? Why did you leave?"

He said, "I got tired, honey, and it was my time," and he started to fade away.

I woke up and ran to the living room where my aunt and mom were, and I told them what happened. My aunt said he crossed over peacefully and started smiling. My aunt Sheila came over to check on us. She was always there. My aunt J was having a hard time sleeping; I knew it was because of Grandad's passing. I was worried about her a lot because I had my mom and my kids, and my brother had his little family, but she was going to be by herself. So, I vowed to myself to continue to build a relationship with her, because even though I wasn't her child, she had always helped us. She made sure we were spoiled on Christmas, when school started, and on our birthdays. Little did I know, that woman would become my best friend.

We stayed in contact through thick and thin. I remember barely seeing her when I was younger, but she used to always come around birthdays, holidays, and the start of school to make sure we got everything we needed. During the hardest death our family experienced, we became closer.

I had my kids, mom, dad, brother, aunts, and close friends. Every day became a little easier. I didn't have to worry about child care because my dad stayed and watched the kids, but I had become irresponsible with my money. I knew that I couldn't call on my Grandad to bail me out anymore, but my best friend D was always there to help me with my kids no matter what the cost. One day D and I were sitting in the car, and I was telling him to watch his back because people around him envied him.

He said, "Shawn, if any nigga tries me, they're gon' have to kill me," and he laughed.

He had a funny laugh. We chilled for a long time that night just talking and laughing. A couple of months went by, and it was his birthday. He wanted me to go out with him, but I declined. He started thinking that I was acting funny and stopped calling me. A couple of months went by, and I messaged him on Facebook to come see me. He declined at first, but he pulled up at my apartment anyway.

We sat and talked for a long time that night. He told me he wanted to stop doing what he was doing and get his CDL license to get his life on track. I told him he could do whatever he put his mind to. On January 28 at 4:30 p.m., he called and told me to come to the Nina Mart store because he had something for me. I went to the store, he got out of the car, and he asked me to be honest with him. He asked if my youngest child was his since we messed around about the time I got pregnant. However, at the time we were messing around, I was still with Troy. He said he just needed to know. I told him I was sure she wasn't his, but that we could get a DNA test. We agreed on Friday that we would get a DNA test done. He gave me $200 and told me to get the kids whatever they needed.

He said, "I'm gone call you tonight to come chill."

I said, "Okay, be careful. I will check on you later."

We hugged, and he left. I went and got my kids snacks from Walmart and went home and cooked. Later that night, he called around 8 p.m. I didn't answer because I was asleep. He sent a text message telling me to come to where he was at in Eastwood. When I woke up around 11 p.m., I called him, and he didn't answer the phone. I texted and Face-book-messaged him telling I would come, but if he didn't respond, I wasn't coming. I kept calling and was getting a little worried because he wasn't active on Facebook for a couple of hours, which wasn't like him. I knew every day he would call around 2 a.m. before he went home. But he didn't call, so I got mad and went to sleep. I woke up the next morning to no missed calls or text messages from him. I got dressed, went over to my aunt Sheila's house, logged into my Facebook, and saw a post that said "RIP D."

I dropped my phone and looked at the TV. The news said he was found dead after be-ing shot that night. I couldn't believe it, so my aunt Sheila, my cousin, and I drove to where he was killed, and I saw people standing out-side the house. Police were everywhere and there was yellow tape all over the place. I just started crying and couldn't believe that he had been killed. He helped everybody no matter the cost. Who would do this to D?

As the days passed, his story was on the

news and in the newspaper. I could only imagine how his mother and daughters felt, as well as his family and friends. He was a loving and caring person no matter what. Now, I'd lost my grandad and one of my best friends. I didn't think I would see the day when D was lying in a casket, cold and lifeless. The date of his wake, I wasn't going to go, but I had to. As I entered the church building, I knew my best friend was gone and wasn't coming back. In my head, our conversations replayed.

He always said, "Shawn, no matter what, keep your head up and get money and stay true."

As I walked in and saw him lying there in all white with his braids, I knew he was really gone, and I would never hear or see him again. I spoke and said good things about him, like how he got me and my mom back on good terms and how he was always there no matter how mad I made him. He was truly one of the best people God placed in my life, and he was gone. I looked over at his mom, and I could feel her pain, but she tried to hold it together and stay strong.

I remember he used to say, "Pull up, Shawn. I'm at my T-Jones's house down the street."

Until this day, I read our Facebook messages, and I kept my old phone with our last messages and calls for memories. On the day of his funeral, the entire city was there. Over a thousand cars were there celebrating. It was packed as we made it to Cedar Hill to lay him to rest. His mom let out a cry when they were lowering his casket. I couldn't imagine the pain she was going through in losing a child. On the ride home from the funeral, I turned on the radio and "Got to be a G" came on by Lil Keke. I smiled and knew he was in a better place. He made a difference in my life, and I miss him so much. That saying "you never know what you have until it's gone," is right.

I was living without my Grandad and now D. I missed them so much. I pulled up to my aunt Sheila's house, and she was cooking and cursing people out. She loved talking crap, but at the end of the day, she was right about everything. The next couple of days I was getting into it with Troy, and he was sending pictures with D and my youngest daughter picture side by side. He was asking if she was his daughter, and I stopped responding because I didn't want to hear or see that right now. At the end of the day, I took care of all my kids like a mother was supposed to, so I didn't care about anything else but them. We tried to be cordial, but it didn't work because we would always end up fighting. He texted me and told me if he couldn't be with us, nobody could. My aunt Sheila called to make sure we were okay and told me that Troy was going to kill us.

She said, "Shawn, he didn't look right. He looked like he was on some drugs, and he said he gon' kill y'all."

I was scared knowing that he could kill us at any given time. I still had the gun my grandad had given me before he passed away, so I went and got some bullets just in case I had to protect myself and my kids. Troy kept calling and texting me, and then he started knocking on the door. My mom was at work, so it was just me and the kids there. I ran and got my gun and put my kids in the closet. I told Trey to make sure they stayed in the closet. No matter what he heard, I told him to not come out until he heard the police.

Troy started kicking the door, and I closed the closet door. I stood in front of the closet door and prayed that he wouldn't kick the door in. I clocked my gun. As I walked to the living room, the front door swung open, and he stepped through the door. He had a gun in his hands, and he pointed the gun at me.

As I pointed my gun back, I saw out of the corner of my eye that Trey was standing in the middle of the hallway crying and yelling for me to

He walked toward me with his gun pointed at me, and then he cocked his gun. I saw my life flash before me and just shot my gun.

not let him kill us. He walked toward me with his gun pointed at me, and then he cocked his gun. I saw my life flash before me and just shot my gun.

He yelled, "Bitch, you shot me!"

Trey ran over to me, and I dropped my gun and grabbed him. The police were making their way to my door so I ran to the closet and grabbed my girls. As I walked back to the living room, the police were getting him off the floor. I had shot him in his leg. The paramedic put him on the stretcher, and the policeman asked me what happened. I showed him the missed calls and the text messages, and by that time, my aunt Sheila was there and told him what Troy had told her.

I couldn't believe he was going to kill us.

They took the gun for evidence and took him to the hospital. I still don't know until this day how he was released from the hospital and didn't go to jail. The detectives kept in touch with me and in June 2015, he was caught and went to jail. I tried to stay in contact with his mother, and my aunt Sheila would warn me that she'd try to have my kids taken again.

I got a call from CPS stating they had been informed that my dad was sexually assaulting my kids and using drugs around them. It's like I couldn't catch a break, but I had my family there to back me up. The day the CPS lady came out to see what was going on, we were there together. They asked my kids questions without me in the room and evaluated them. I couldn't believe this, because my dad would never do anything like that. He was pissed off because he loved his grandkids. After they spoke with my kids, we all sat in the living room, and they tested my dad for crack/cocaine. He told him he was still using but never around the kids.

He told them he would only use on the weekends, which was when my dad would leave. I knew my dad was using, but that was his drug habit since I was a little girl. I didn't judge him because I knew his heart, and he would never let anything happen to my kids in his care. Since he had voluntarily told them about his habit, the CPS caseworker said that she would throw out the case, but she suggested I put them in day care because cases like this never end well. She threw out all charges. I understood the concern and placed my kids in day care where my mother worked out.

I vowed to myself I would never speak to Troy or his mother again.

I didn't know if they plotted that together or not, but I didn't want to risk having her take my kids again.

With just me paying all the bills, day care was becoming expensive. I called the CPS caseworker and told her that I couldn't afford day care.

She told me the case was closed but if anything happened to my kids in my dad's care, I would be held responsible. I trusted my dad, and Pam pitched and watched them for me as well. One day, my aunt J came over and asked if I was ready to move into a house in Mansfield. She said her tenants were moving out, and she needed to place someone in there whom she trusted. I told her I was ready to be responsible and move into the house. We agreed the move-in date would be November 1, 2016. I told my aunt Pam, and she talked crap as usual.

She said, "Shawn, make sure you clean up and keep them kids fed every day or I'm gon' kick your butt."

I laughed, and she said, "You gon' come get me on the weekends?"

I told her I would. On Mother's Day, I spent time with my mom and kids, and then I left and went over to see one of my best friends, Gina. She said Sheila called her crying, saying no one had called, and she wanted me to come get her. Gina went and got her, and her stomach had gotten swollen, but we didn't pay any mind because it was normal for her. One minute she was swollen, and the next she was good. We helped her up the stairs, and we had a good time. I called my cousin Jasmine, her daughter, to come over. Jasmine came over, and Sheila was happy. Gina cooked, and we played dominoes and had a good time.

Chapter 5

SELF LOVE AND HAPPINESS

In June 2016, Sheila went to the hospital, and she called me from the observation room. When I asked her what was going on, she said everything was good and she would be home in a couple of days. When she made it home, she was still swollen but she kept drinking and having a good time every day.

On July 3, a day before my birthday, Sheila called and told me to come over.

When I got there, she wanted to see what I was doing for my birthday on July 4th. We laughed like normal but deep down she was acting strange and saying strange things. However, I didn't pay attention to it. She said she wanted to make sure she had the right number, so she called my phone while I was sitting there and left a crazy voicemail.

We laughed, but I should have been paying attention to her strange behavior, because she had just called me to come over so I know she had the right number. It's like she was losing her memory or something, but again we didn't pay any attention to it. She wanted her hair done for the 4th, and Rhonda, her youngest daughter, put in a clip-on ponytail for her.

All day and even on my birthday, she kept saying her head was hurting. She said she had been taking her Advil, but it was barely working. On my birthday, she walked to my apartment but she barely made it up the stairs. Trey helped her up the stairs, and she sat down by my window and drank some beer. She just kept saying her head was hurting and she was getting dizzy. I suggested that she lie down and told her I would bring her a plate from the BBQ my brother was throwing for me. She agreed, and my dad had to drive her to her apartment.

She said, "Shawn, make sure you get me a plate, baby. I'm gon' be here waiting on you."

I told her I would. We made it to my BBQ

at my brother's house, and an hour later, I saw Sheila walking up the street with her niece.

She was struggling trying to walk because her feet had gotten so big and swollen.

I was so pissed because she didn't need to be outside at all; she needed to be resting. As my brother and I grabbed her, I asked her what she was doing.

She said, "You know I had to be here with you for your birthday, baby. I couldn't miss it."

I kept an eye on her and made sure she had eaten. She said she was feeling dizzy again, so my brother told her niece to take her home.

When the party was over, I went to her apartment and knocked on the door. The dining room light was on, but nobody answered the front door so I went around to her back door and knocked. I tried to look through the window. I heard her tell me to come back later because she was in the bathroom. I asked her if she was sure. I was going to wait until I saw that she was okay with my own two eyes, but she said she was sure. So I went home and lay down because I was tipsy.

The next day, I got up and called her phone. She didn't answer, but it was still early so I didn't think anything was wrong. I went to work, and around 11 a.m., Jasmine called crying and said she had found Sheila hanging on the side of the bed with her eyes rolling back. I panicked and ran out of work.

I knew I was not about to lose one of the most important people I had left.

I couldn't deal with another death. My grandad died in February 2014, D in January 2015, and now I might be losing my baby right after my birthday.

When I got to the hospital, they said she had suffered from an aneurysm and that her brain had shifted and needed surgery. I knew from that point my baby was gone, but I kept my faith and stayed strong. After the brain surgery, she was out for a couple of days. The doctors said she was making progress, so I just prayed and visited her every chance I got. She eventually got better and was released from the hospital into rehab. We were all so happy she survived that scare.

During that time, I slowed down and went to see her, because I just wanted her to come home. I wanted us all to go over her house like good old days and play dominoes and have fun while she got drunk and showed out. But as the month went by, April told me that her seizures had returned and she couldn't eat. She ended up back in the hospital, so the kids and I went up to the hospital on her birthday, July 28, to see her. She was kind of in and out, but she was talking and knew who we all were. I stayed there for about two hours, and I kissed her and left.

August went by, and she was in the same condition so they decided to move her to hospice care to make her comfortable. At the time, I really didn't comprehend what was going on because I still knew she was going to be okay. I didn't understand why they had placed her in hospice care, and I felt the doctors had given up on her because she was an alcoholic and they didn't want to deal with it. I didn't care what addiction she had, she was my baby, and I knew in my heart she was going to make it out of it. On Memorial Day, September 5, April came and got me and told me I needed to go see her. I didn't want to see her like that because that wasn't how my Sheila was.

When I got to the hospice place and entered her room, I said, "Girl, get up. We got to get on this bus and go to East Texas!"

She used to always say she wanted to get

the bus and go to East Texas for vacation. She opened her eyes as soon as she heard my voice. She stared at me for a long time trying to say something, but her mouth was so dry she couldn't get it out. I knew she liked music so I put on Johnnie Taylor's "Soul Heaven," and she closed her eyes. She laid there for a minute, and then I noticed her eyes were twitching.

I told Jasmine, who told the doctors, and they said they were just making Sheila comfortable until she passed.

I still kept my faith that she was going to make it. They said she was holding on to the fluid and she was releasing it, meaning her liver hardened up and wasn't working anymore. I couldn't take that. I didn't care what those doctors said; Sheila was going to be okay, and she was going to be back home in no time.

The next day, Jasmine told me to get Rhonda and come up there because they were going to give her a pill that might help release the fluids. If the pill worked, she was going to be fine; but if it didn't work by that night, then she was going to pass within hours or the next day. As we made it up there, I went in the room and talked to her. I kissed her hand and prayed over her. My faith was still strong that everything was going to be okay. As her two oldest children, Jasmine and the kids, Rhonda, and I sat there, it was getting late. The doctors told us the pill didn't work, and they gave her hours to live. We all kept our faith up, saying she was going to make it, she wasn't going to pass, she was going to be okay.

Her best friend started crying and said, "Sheila, wake up girl. You know you're not ready. We love you. We can't live without you."

As everyone started to leave, I kissed her one last time and left.

As I dropped Pooh off, I just couldn't sleep, so I just drove without a destination. Jasmine called me crying around 12, and then Rhonda called crying. I knew right then my Sheila Gram was gone. I just drove until I had to pull over and cry. I couldn't believe this was happening. Three years back to back I'd lost an important person in my life and didn't understand why.

My aunt Sheila passed away on September 7, 2016. Jasmine stepped up to the plate and took care of everything. She had to gather money help bury her because her life insurance had lapsed. She got everything taken care of and dressed her nicely for the wake and funeral. I was out of it—I couldn't believe Sheila was gone just like that. Whatever they told her in June 2016 at the hospital, she didn't tell us. I guess she didn't want us to worry. At the wake, everyone got up and spoke about her. But what stuck in my head was what her grandchild Jordan said. She stood up there staring at the casket crying.

She said, "Why, G-Mama, why? I didn't want this to happen to you!"

I cried, and my heart and soul were hurting for that baby because Jordan knew her G-Mama loved her to death. The next day at her funeral, all her kids were there, and all of us were crying. It was my time to say my goodbyes, and as I walked up there, I thought I was going to be strong, give her a kiss, and go sit back down. It didn't work that way, however. As I saw her lying there, I imagined my Grandad and D, and now Sheila in a casket—cold and lifeless. I leaned down to give her a kiss and broke down.

I fell to my knees crying.

I started yelling, "No, Sheila! Please come back. Please, we can't live without you!"

I felt as if I'd lost a mother figure, because she treated me like one of her children. I was at my breaking point, and if I didn't get help, I didn't know what I was going to do.

I had to take a stress leave from work because my doctor said I needed to be under psychological care. He said I needed to come in every week until he felt I was better. He tried to put me on meds, but I didn't feel right when I started taking them.

On November 1, 2016, I moved into my house. The only thing I could think about was Sheila and how proud she would be to see that I finally got my house.

She used to always say, "Shawn, these kids need a house with a backyard. You need to get them away from those damn roach-infested apartments," and she would burst out laughing.

My brother and aunt helped me move in, and my mom and dad moved in as well. I noticed that my dad didn't like it out there, so I didn't know how long he would stay. He started complaining more and more, and I knew that I had to get babysitter for my kids because he could leave at any given time. It worked out for a couple of months, but my mom didn't keep up with our agreement financially. Months would go by, and I would have to pay the mortgage, light bill, water bill, etc., with no help. Although three adults were living there, I was taking care of everything by myself. I had to go back to work because my paid leave dropped to 50%, and I couldn't afford to pay everything. My mom still didn't help. Christmas came, and I made sure I bought my kids what they wanted. It was our first Christmas in our house, and I loved it. We decorated the tree and everything. I started to notice that my kids were all I needed. I grew tired of feeling like I owed my mom and trying to keep her happy when she only wanted to make sure my dad wouldn't leave.

In February 2017, she got her income taxes and still didn't help with anything in the house. I had gotten a low amount because of my student loans, but I still managed to make sure we had beds. I bought a washer and dryer because we needed it.

My best friend at the time invited me on a trip to Florida. I went on the trip and had one of the best times of my life. As I was sitting on the beach, I started thinking about writing a book about my life. *I felt so alive sitting on that beach. Looking at all that water, my spirit was calm and cool, and I was at peace.* I never knew what peace felt like until I went to Florida.

As soon as I returned home from my trip, all the drama started again. I had my aunt and brother saying that my dad and mom were going to leave, but I didn't believe them. Months went by, and my mom was paying $80-$100 per month. I couldn't understand why she couldn't keep money to help with the bills. In May, she said she was going to pay the light bill and didn't. I had paid all the bills, got some things for the house, and started school shopping for my kids because I didn't want to wait until the last minute to get all three of my kids their things.

It was going to be hard, but she didn't understand that.

She spent the light bill money, and I got an email with a disconnect date.

I wasn't going to get paid in time to pay it, so I had to pawn my baby's PlayStation 4. He was crying, but I didn't know what else to do. I was fed up that time—I was done. I'd rather struggle by myself than have people in my house who didn't care about helping me. So, I sat her down and told her that my dad had to go. She was crying and said he could leave but she would stay. I told her we were good at maintaining the bills together in the apartment before he came back in the picture. I thought she understood that, but she didn't. My dad and I got into it because she told me he was taking her money. I asked him why he would do that if he knew she needed to help pay bills, and he started yelling back. I told him to get his stuff and get out.

Then, my mom started crying and saying I was telling her to leave, too. She knew I didn't tell her to leave, and my brother was there and told her I didn't say that.

At the end of the day, she wanted to leave with my dad even though she knew he couldn't do anything for her.

It's like she couldn't live without him.

I'm 29 years old, and she has been choosing him over me since I was born. Yes, it hurt to see them leave because they had my nephew with them, and I didn't know where they were going. They left in May 2017, and I haven't heard from them since.

My life started taking a turn for the better. I had gotten to know myself, and I was at peace. It was just me and kids. I had gained that peace when I was on the beach in Florida, and I didn't ever want to lose it. As I look back on my life, I still consider myself very blessed. I was able to make it out alive from those toxic and abusive relationships.

My story is for everyone to read and learn from. When you learn to love yourself, you will see your value. **Everyone grows apart, and that is okay, but you are responsible for your own happiness**. A wise man taught me to always think positively no matter what.

Yes, times are still hard being a single mother to three kids, but if I can survive from my past and create a better future, so can you!

Always think positively, believe in yourself, and love yourself enough to let go of the toxic relationships. There are always signs, but we just look over them because we love those people unconditionally. However, love yourself enough to leave, and live your life happily. Remember, you only get one!

Many of you may think I was a victim, but I don't look at myself that way because I had two choices, and I chose to stay. I look at this experience as a lesson, and I've learned from it. Self-love is only something *you* can experience, and once you do, you will not allow anything, and I mean anything, to interrupt it. Remember to live your life for yourself, not for this world, and always remain positive!

ABOUT THE AUTHOR

VANESSA FARR has longed to share her personal life story about how she survived the entrapment of domestic violence. She was inspired to write her novel after losing a friend to domestic abuse, a situation Vanessa was blessed to live from. Vanessa hopes that the dark memories referenced in her book will help teenagers and women who have suffered from the same prison of domestic violence to overcome their shackles of abuse like she did. Vanessa currently resides in Arlington, Texas.

J. Kenkade
PUBLISHING

Our Motto
"Transforming Life Stories"

Publish Your Book With Us

Our All-Inclusive Publishing Package
Professional Proofreading & Editing
Book Formatting & Cover Design
Manuscript Writing Assistance
Author Classes & More

For Manuscript Submission or other inquiries:
www.jkenkadepublishing.com
(501) 482-1000

J. Kenkade
PUBLISHING

Also Available from
J. Kenkade Publishing

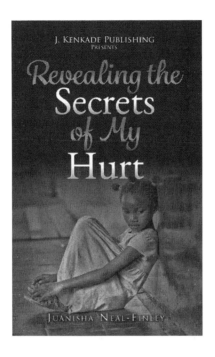

ISBN: 978-1-944486-13-6
Visit www.jkenkade.com
Author: Juanisha Neal-Finley

"Revealing the Secrets of My Hurt" is a life story of a young girl tormented by an abusive family. Young Cindy rewrites her experiences with a mother introduced to drugs, sexual abuse from her father, and death. Cindy reveals how strong God can make anyone in the midst of Satan's schemes. Experience her journey in, "Revealing the Secrets of My Hurt."

Also Available from
J. Kenkade Publishing

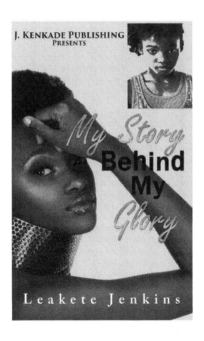

ISBN: 978-1-944486-14-3
Visit www.jkenkade.com
Author: Leakete Jenkins

The story of a young girl born with medical issues and throughout her childhood, suffered molestation, tried to commit suicide, was involved in an abusive relationship, and felt as if no one cared for her. This book will invite you into a story that is so heart-breaking, but will also show you that through any obstacle, God will see you through.

Also Available from
J. Kenkade Publishing

ISBN: 978-1-944486-04-4
Visit www.jkenkade.com
Author: Rahsaan Aki Taylor

A dose of inspiration for every day of your life. Each day, we are faced with challenges that we must conquer and overcome. The contents of this book will help you maintain, stay afloat, and solve some of your troubles. There is a skill, a strategy, and an art to living a prosperous and peaceful life.

Made in the USA
Middletown, DE
29 March 2023

27161834R00071